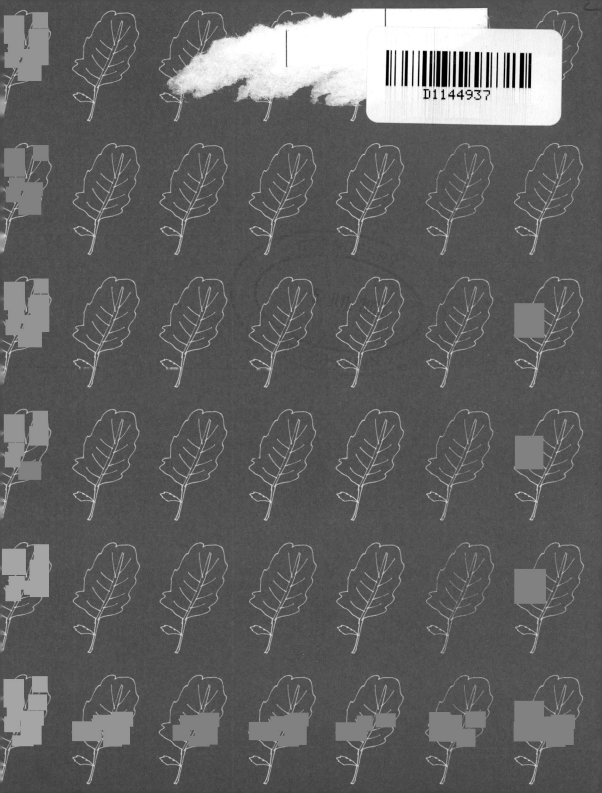

GREENS

THE GOODNESS OF
GREENS

40 INCREDIBLE NUTRIENT-PACKED RECIPES

EDITED BY **CLAIRE ROGERS**
KYLE BOOKS

CONTENTS

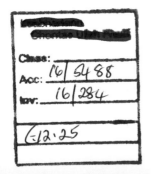

GREENS ARE GREAT

From dark leafy iron-filled kale to bright, crisp beans and springy, vitamin-rich watercress, there are so many ways to enjoy eating your greens. Once relegated to the side of the meal, here they take centre stage and are celebrated for their delicious, nutritious goodness.

Whether you're a dedicated veg-eater or just want to up your intake, you will find plenty of recipes to whet your appetite in the following pages, divided into chapters arranged by type: Beans & Legumes (peas, mangetout, green beans, broad beans); Leafy Greens (spinach, watercress, chard, lettuce, rocket); and Brassicas (kale, cabbage, broccoli, Brussels sprouts).

You'll find recipes for all these green veggies and interesting ways to prepare them. Cabbage leaves used as wraps, raw sprouts in salad, a gorgeous green salad incorporating no less than four different greens, plus soups, salads, juices, stir-fries and, yes, even kale crisps (see page 67)! There is so much to choose from.

THE GOODNESS OF GREENS

Greens, particularly dark leafy ones such as kale and spinach, are packed full of vitamins and minerals that help maintain both a healthy appearance (skin and hair) and healthy insides (your bones and your gut among others). Studies have suggested that vegetables rich in antioxidants and phytonutrients, such as cruciferous vegetables (broccoli, cabbage, etc.) and dark leafy greens are linked to a reduced risk of heart disease and even some cancers.

Fresh is best

Vegetables lose nutrients from the moment they are picked, so the fresher the better. It can be several days from when they are picked to when they are stocked on supermarket shelves. Frozen veg are a good alternative if you can't find fresh. These are generally frozen very soon after they are picked, which helps preserve the nutrients. Some supermarkets also stock 'living salads' which can be placed on a windowsill and harvested as needed.

BUYING THE BEST

In order to get the most vitamins and minerals from your greens, you need to buy the freshest produce possible. Farmers' markets are excellent sources of organic, pesticide-free veg, but you can also grow your own.

Top tips for buying good greens

♦ Always buy as fresh as possible.
♦ Avoid anything with wilting leaves or leaves starting to turn yellow.
♦ Choose greens with the brightest, crispest colours.
♦ Check stalks – you want them to be firm, not bendy.

STORING

Most green vegetables are best stored in the fridge to keep them fresh for longer. Some will last longer than others; beans and greens with tightly-packed leaves (broccoli, Brussels sprouts, cabbage) usually last up to a week; soft, looser-leaved greens (kale, Swiss chard, watercress) will only last about 3 days. If you store your greens in plastic bags, make sure there are holes to allow airflow. There is no need to wash broccoli, peas and lettuce before storing in the fridge; simply wash when you are ready to use them.

BEANS & LEGUMES

SPRING PEA SOUP

*GLUTEN-FREE

Fresh peas are best for this soup, as they have enough body to yield a creamier texture. Better yet are petits pois – spring peas harvested very young and tender. Serve this hot or chilled to suit the weather outside.

Serves 4

675g fresh peas, shucked
  (reserve pea pods)
1 medium onion, diced
3 cloves garlic, chopped
1 medium potato, peeled
  and diced
1 litre gluten-free vegetable
  stock
8 ice cubes
60ml crème fraîche
Sea salt
Lemon juice, to taste

To serve
10g mint leaves,
  julienned
12 pea flowers
6 pea shoots
1 tablespoon lemon zest,
  finely julienned

1. In a medium saucepan over a high heat, blanch the shucked peas in boiling salted water until their colour brightens, or 20–30 seconds. Drain the peas and immediately plunge them into a bowl of iced water. After the peas have chilled, drain and set aside.

2. In a medium saucepan over a medium-high heat, combine the reserved pea pods, onion, garlic, potato and stock. Boil until the stock is reduced to three-quarters of its original volume and the potato is very tender, or about 40 minutes.

3. Transfer to a blender or food processor. Add half of the reserved peas. Blend until velvety smooth, adding water if the soup is too thick to easily purée. Strain through a fine colander. Add the ice cubes and crème fraîche and stir until the ice cubes have melted. Season with salt and lemon juice and place in the fridge to fully chill, about 1 hour. To serve the soup warm, return it to the saucepan and warm fully over a low heat, for 10–15 minutes.

4. Divide the soup into four soup bowls. Top each with the mint leaves, pea flowers and shoots, and lemon zest. Serve immediately.

When making chilled soup, add ice cubes at the end to cool the soup quickly and thin it out. It helps to keep the colour of green vegetable soups brighter.

PEA, MINT & PINE NUT SOUP *DAIRY-FREE

Pine nuts give the soup a luxuriously creamy texture and the mint makes it taste like a bowlful of spring.

Serves 1

120g frozen or fresh peas
1 garlic clove, peeled
175ml chicken stock or water
2 tablespoons pine nuts,
    toasted
1 tablespoon olive oil
A handful of fresh
    mint leaves
Sea salt and freshly
    ground black pepper

1. Place the peas, garlic and stock in a saucepan. Bring to the boil. Turn off the heat and let it sit for 3 minutes.

2. Grind the pine nuts to a paste in a blender or with a pestle and mortar. Trickle in the olive oil and give it a good mix.

3. Place the peas in a blender with the pine nut paste and fresh mint. Whizz to a smooth purée. Add more stock if needed. If you want a smoother soup, pass it through a sieve. Season to taste and serve.

BEETROOT, PEA & WATERCRESS *GLUTEN-FREE

This salad has so many flavours and textures going on that the added slivers of roast lamb are like the icing on top.

Serves 4

2 beetroot, cut into
  2cm wedges
A few glugs of olive oil
A drizzle of honey
300g frozen peas
100g watercress
Sea salt and freshly ground
  black pepper
Juice and zest of ½ lemon
Boiled new potatoes
125g cold roast lamb,
  chopped

For the dressing
75g natural or Greek yogurt
1 garlic clove, finely minced
4 tablespoons grated
  cucumber
A few fresh mint leaves

1. Splash some olive oil into a large frying pan. Add the beetroot and sauté until tender, 10–15 minutes. Drizzle the honey over. Set aside to cool.

2. Place the peas in a colander and rinse in warm water until defrosted.

3. Divide the watercress between the plates. Season with salt and pepper, drizzle the lemon juice and olive oil over, scatter with lemon zest and toss to combine. Set the beetroot pieces among the watercress, then add the potatoes. Sprinkle the peas over the top. Gently mix through the watercress leaves. Dot the lamb over the top.

4. For the dressing, mix the yogurt with the garlic, cucumber and mint, and season to taste. Drizzle this over the top of the salad and serve.

GREEN PEA RAVIOLI
*VEGETARIAN

Fresh peas are obviously a lot more work for the preparation of these ravioli, but really do make a difference.

Serves 6–8

For the pasta dough
250g '00' flour
2 large eggs, beaten
1 large egg yolk, beaten
1 tablespoon olive oil

For the green pea ravioli
300g shelled peas (or frozen)
20g mint leaves
100g good-quality ricotta
　cheese, well drained
2 spring onions, finely chopped
Sea salt and freshly ground
　black pepper
1 tablespoon lemon juice

For the saffron butter sauce
150ml good vegetable stock
100ml double cream
Good pinch of quality saffron
　(or ½ teaspoon powdered)
40g unsalted butter, chilled
　and cut into small pieces

For the truffled beetroot salad
1 tablespoon balsamic vinegar
Pinch of sugar
½ tablespoon truffle oil
1 medium beetroot, cooked,
　peeled and very thinly sliced
1 truffle, very thinly sliced
　(optional)
50g pea shoots

1. Blend all the pasta ingredients and 1 tablespoon of water in a food-processor for a few seconds to mix – do not overwork the dough. Remove, then knead the dough until soft and pliable. Wrap in clingfilm and put in the fridge for 1 hour to rest.

2. Cook the peas in just enough boiling water to cover, for 5–6 minutes until tender and then drain, reserving 100ml of the cooking water. Refresh in iced water, drain and dry them well. Place in a food-processor with the mint, ricotta and spring onions and blend to a coarse purée. Remove to a bowl, season to taste and add the lemon juice.

3. Roll out the pasta into thin sheets, then brush a sheet with water and place tablespoons of the pea-ricotta mixture on it, about 5cm apart in rows. Cover with a second sheet of pasta, press down gently around the fillings, then cut the pasta into squares. Check to ensure the edges are well sealed, place on a lightly floured tray and leave to dry for 20 minutes.

4. For the saffron butter, heat the vegetable stock, reserved pea cooking liquid, cream and saffron in a pan and simmer until the liquid has reduced by half. Remove from the heat, whisk in the chilled butter, season to taste and then finely strain.

5. Cook the ravioli in plenty of simmering water for 3–4 minutes until al dente, then remove with a slotted spoon and drain well.

6. For the salad, whisk together the vinegar, sugar and oil, add the beetroot and truffle and adjust the seasoning; mix well.

7. Divide the ravioli between four serving dishes, pour over the saffron sauce, top with the beetroot salad and pea shoots and serve immediately.

ORIENTAL CRAYFISH WITH MANGETOUT

*DAIRY-FREE

Crayfish is considered a huge pest in our waters, as the American Crayfish is eating much of our native river life, so it seems only right that we do our bit to control this pest by encouraging you to put it on your plate!

Serves 6

For the salad
200g black rice
200g mangetout
100g dried egg noodles
800g cooked, peeled
   crayfish tails
½ Chinese cabbage, shredded
1 red pepper, deseeded and
   diced into 1cm cubes
2 spring onions, finely
   chopped
100g toasted flaked almonds
2 carrots, cut into ribbons
   with a ribbon peeler
1 cucumber, cut into ribbons
   with a ribbon peeler

For the dressing
1 tablespoon finely
   chopped fresh coriander
3 tablespoons rice wine
   vinegar
2 tablespoons soy sauce
Juice of 1 lime
5cm piece of root ginger,
   peeled and grated
1 teaspoon sugar
1 tablespoon olive oil

1. Preheat the oven to 180°C/fan 160°C/gas mark 4.

2. Place the rice in a medium pan of boiling water and cook for 15 minutes or until soft and cooked. Drain and rinse with cold water. Set aside. Meanwhile, blanch the mangetout in a pan of salted, boiling water for 4 minutes, and drain and rinse with cold water.

3. Place the noodles on a baking tray and bake them until golden brown. Leave them to cool and then crush them with your hands.

4. Combine all the dressing ingredients in a small jug, and whisk until thoroughly mixed. Place all the salad ingredients in a large serving bowl and stir to combine. Add the dressing... badabing!

MANGETOUT & ARTICHOKE SALAD

*DAIRY-FREE

There is nothing to beat this crisp, fruity salad. Serve it as a dinner-party knockout or just a lazy weekend treat.

Serves 4 as a side

250g poivrade artichokes
150g Jerusalem artichokes
250g mangetout

For the dressing
Zest of ½ orange, cut
   into long shreds
Juice of ½ orange
1 teaspoon wholegrain
   mustard
1½ tablespoons
   champagne vinegar
2½ tablespoons virgin
   olive oil
4 tablespoons walnut oil
Salt and freshly
   ground black pepper

1. Prepare the poivrade artichokes by removing the stalks and trimming 1cm off the tops of the leaves. As they are very young and tender, no other preparation is required.

2. Peel the Jerusalem artichokes. Cook the poivrade and Jerusalem artichokes in separate pans of boiling salted water for 8–10 minutes or until tender, then drain. Blanch the mangetout in boiling water for 2 minutes. Drain and refresh under cold water, then drain again.

3. For the dressing, blanch the orange zest in boiling water for 1 minute, then refresh under cold water and drain well. Whisk together all the dressing ingredients, adding seasoning to taste.

4. Place the artichokes in a bowl, pour over the dressing, then add the mangetout. Serve at room temperature.

THAI GREEN VEGETABLE CURRY

*VEGETARIAN *DAIRY-FREE

The addition of sweet pineapple to this vibrant curry gives it a real lift. The green chilli adds a little extra heat but this can be left out if you prefer a more subtly spiced dish.

Serves 6

1 tablespoon rapeseed oil
2 banana shallots, chopped
1 green chilli, deseeded
   and finely chopped
55g Thai green curry paste
75g red lentils
2 leeks, washed and sliced
1 red and 1 yellow pepper,
   deseeded and thickly sliced
300g butternut squash,
   peeled and cubed
200g green beans, trimmed
   and cut into 3cm lengths
300g half-fat coconut milk
220g can pineapple rings,
   drained and cut into chunks
150g spinach leaves
Sea salt and freshly
   ground black pepper

To serve
Thai jasmine rice
A large handful of fresh
   coriander, chopped
80g cashew nuts, toasted
   in a dry pan

1. Heat the rapeseed oil in a large, non-stick pan over a low-medium heat. Add the shallots and green chilli and cook gently for a few minutes. Add the curry paste and cook gently for a further 2 minutes, stirring frequently.

2. Stir the lentils into the paste then add the leeks, peppers, squash, beans and coconut milk. Bring to the boil then lower the heat and simmer, covered, for about 20 minutes, by which time the lentils should be very soft.

3. Stir in the pineapple pieces and add the spinach leaves. Cover the pan and simmer for 2 more minutes, by which time the spinach will have wilted and can be stirred easily into the sauce.

4. Taste and adjust the seasoning. Serve with Thai jasmine rice and top with fresh coriander and toasted cashew nuts.

Sweet potato or even pumpkin can be used in place of butternut squash.

RED TOFU & FRENCH BEANS *VEGETARIAN *DAIRY-FREE

This delicate marinade adds a sweet yet hot coating to the tofu, topping a wonderfully fragrant and fresh salad.

Serves 4

250g pack firm tofu, drained
1 tablespoon honey
2 tablespoons plum sauce
2 tablespoons dark soy sauce
3 teaspoons sweet chilli sauce
325g French beans, topped
  and tailed
2 tablespoons cashew nuts,
  roasted and chopped
2 persimmons, stem removed
  and cut into wedges
Salt and freshly ground
  black pepper
2 tablespoons groundnut
  or vegetable oil

For the dressing
2 tablespoons palm
  or brown sugar
2 tablespoons coarse sea salt
2 garlic cloves, chopped
A good handful of mint leaves
4 hot green chillies,
  deseeded and chopped
1cm piece of root ginger,
  peeled and grated
3 tablespoons vegetarian fish
  sauce (*nuoc mam chay*)
Juice of 8 limes
4 shallots, thinly sliced

1. Cut the tofu in half widthways, then cut both pieces in half horizontally to give four equally thick slices. In a shallow dish combine the honey with the plum, soy and sweet chilli sauces. Place the tofu slices in the marinade and leave to marinate for 2 hours, turning regularly to ensure the tofu is thoroughly coated.

2. For the dressing, melt the sugar in a small pan. Place the salt, garlic and mint in a mortar and lightly pound to a pulp with a pestle. Add the chillies, palm sugar and ginger and pound again. Add the fish sauce, lime juice and shallots and mix well. Leave for 1 hour for the flavours to develop.

3. Cook the beans in a pan of boiling salted water for 2–3 minutes or until just cooked, but still retaining a good bite.

4. Place the beans, cashews and persimmons in a bowl and pour over the prepared dressing. Toss well and season to taste. Remove the tofu from the marinade. Heat a large frying pan with the oil, add the tofu and cook for about 2 minutes on each side until golden and crisp. Place a good pile of the salad on four serving plates, top each with a slice of tofu and serve at once.

GREEN BEANS &
LAMB BROCHETTES
*GLUTEN-FREE

A lemony yogurt dressing forms the base of this salad. If you cut the green beans in half lengthways, this is attractive and makes for a more delicate bite. But this isn't a must, and can be skipped if you prefer not to fuss.

Serves 4

570g boneless leg of lamb
  or lamb shoulder, cut into
  2.5cm cubes
2 garlic cloves, very
  thinly sliced
¾ teaspoon piment
  d'Espelette or ¼ teaspoon
  cayenne pepper
225g green beans, trimmed
  and halved lengthways
225g sugar-snap peas,
  strings removed
2 small red onions, cut into
  1cm wedges, root end intact
5 tablespoons extra virgin
  olive oil
A handful plus 1 tablespoon
  roughly chopped mint

For the dressing
Zest and juice of 1 lemon
75ml Greek yogurt
Sea salt and freshly
  ground black pepper

Metal skewers, or wooden
  skewers soaked in water
  for 10 minutes

1. Place the lamb, lemon zest, garlic and piment d'Espelette into a bowl, then cover and marinate at room temperature for 1 hour or in the fridge overnight. If marinating the meat overnight, bring it to room temperature before grilling.

2. Bring a medium saucepan of salted water to the boil. Add the beans and peas, and cook for about 1½ minutes until just until crisp-tender. Drain, place in a large bowl and set aside.

3. Squeeze 2 tablespoons of lemon juice into a bowl, then add the yogurt and a generous pinch of salt and pepper, stir together and set aside.

4. Preheat the grill to medium-high.

5. Toss the onions with 1½ tablespoons of oil and season generously. Grill, turning

occasionally, until golden and tender, about 5 minutes. Transfer to a plate to cool slightly.

6. Toss the lamb with 1 tablespoon of oil and season generously. Thread the lamb pieces onto the skewers and grill for 3–4 minutes, turning occasionally, until cooked to medium-rare. Transfer to a chopping board and leave to rest for 5 minutes.

7. Meanwhile, add the onion wedges, mint, remaining oil and a generous pinch each of salt and pepper to the bowl with the green bean mixture. Gently toss together, then taste and adjust the seasoning.

8. Spoon the yogurt mixture onto four serving plates and top with the bean salad and skewers.

SPRING SALAD WITH GOAT'S CHEESE *VEGETARIAN

Use this dressing for all manner of salads – tomatoes and basil, chargrilled courgettes and aubergines, sliced avocados or a simple leaf salad. Gremolata is a classic garnish for osso bucco but you can also scatter it over grilled meats, vegetables or fish for an instant lift. Try to buy peas and broad beans still in the pod rather than in ready-prepared packs – they'll be fresher and more flavoursome.

Serves 4 as a starter or light lunch

A large bunch of asparagus
200g podded peas
200g podded broad beans
75g baby leaf spinach
A handful of pea shoots
4 slices of sourdough bread
200g ash-covered young
   goat's cheese log
Sea salt flakes and freshly
   ground black pepper

For the gremolata
2 garlic cloves, finely chopped
4 tablespoons finely chopped
   flat-leaf parsley
Fine strips of zest from
   an unwaxed lemon
2 tablespoons chopped
   pitted green olives

For the lemon dressing
Juice of 1 lemon
4 tablespoons extra virgin
   olive oil
1 teaspoon Dijon mustard
1 teaspoon clear honey

1. Trim the woody ends of the asparagus and cut into 5–6cm lengths. Bring a saucepan of salted water to the boil and blanch the asparagus for 3 minutes or until tender, then refresh in a bowl of iced water. Blanch the peas in the same pan for 1–2 minutes and add to the asparagus. Cook the broad beans in the same water for 1–2 minutes and then drain. Rinse under cold water and then slip each bean from its outer jacket to reveal the bright green, tender bean inside. Drain all the veggies and pat dry on kitchen paper.

2. To make the gremolata, combine all the ingredients in a small bowl and season.

3. Next make the dressing. Squeeze the juice from the lemon into a bowl, add the olive oil and mustard and whisk to combine. Taste and add the honey, then season.

4. Toss the beans, peas and asparagus in the dressing and arrange on plates with the baby leaf spinach and pea shoots.

5. Toast the sourdough on both sides under the grill. Slice the goat's cheese into 1cm-thick discs and place one slice on each piece of toast. Flash the cheese under the grill again until it starts to soften. Spoon the gremolata alongside, drizzle with a little more oil and serve immediately with the salad.

BROAD BEAN & BLUE CHEESE PIZZA *VEGETARIAN

This fennel sauce is also a delicious base for a seaweed pizza, or a kale, spinach or broccoli pizza. It also freezes perfectly so make the full amount and use as required.

Makes 1 pizza
(Dough makes 4 × 150g balls;
can be frozen)

For the dough
225ml cold tap water
10g fresh yeast
450g strong Italian flour,
    such as Tipo 00 or strong
    baker's flour, plus extra
    for dusting
10g dairy salt

For the fennel sauce
1 tablespoon extra virgin
    olive oil
2 onions, thinly sliced
3 garlic cloves, crushed
5 bulbs of fennel, thinly sliced
Sea salt and freshly ground
    black pepper

For the pizza
20 broad beans
Semolina, for sprinkling
1 teaspoon extra virgin
    olive oil
A pinch of Maldon sea salt
8 cubes of blue cheese,
    approx. 1cm
A large handful of grated
    mozzarella
1 teaspoon finely chopped
    flat-leaf parsley, to serve
Lemon wedges, to serve

1. First make the pizza dough: Put the water into the bowl of a food processor. Crumble the yeast into the flour and add to the water along with the salt. Mix for 5 minutes at a medium speed. Leave the dough to rest for 5 minutes, then mix for a further 20 minutes. The dough should be smooth and stick to the side of the mixing bowl.

2. Put the dough in an airtight container four times bigger than the dough. Refrigerate for at least 6 hours, preferably overnight.

3. Sprinkle a work surface with a little flour, then weigh and divide the dough into four 150g pieces using a small knife. Knead the dough into round balls roughly the size of tennis balls, transfer to a tray, sprinkle with flour and refrigerate for 6 hours. Remove from the fridge 1 hour before you cook the pizza.

4. Meanwhile, make the fennel sauce: heat the oil in a pan, add the onions and garlic and sweat until soft but not coloured. Add the fennel slices and 600ml water, then season and simmer for 25 minutes or until soft. Blend until smooth. Taste and correct the seasoning, if necessary.

5. Preheat the oven to 240°C/ fan 220°C/gas mark 9. Blanch the broad beans in boiling water for 2 minutes. Drain, refresh under cold running water and set aside

6. Roll the pizza dough into a 25cm circle. Sprinkle a little semolina over a large baking tray and put the pizza base on top. Drizzle the olive oil over the base of the pizza and sprinkle with the salt. Spread 150ml of the fennel sauce over the base. Scatter over the broad beans and blue cheese and top with the mozzarella.

7. Bake in the oven for 10–12 minutes, or until the base is crisp and the top is bubbly and golden. Sprinkle with parsley and serve immediately, with lemon wedges.

FREEKEH & BROAD BEAN SALAD *VEGETARIAN *DAIRY-FREE

Earthy, slightly smoky, nutty and nutrient-rich, freekeh (pronounced free-ka) is a fantastic grain for salads and side dishes. Look for it in Middle Eastern food shops and online. If freekeh is unavailable, try barley or wholewheat pasta. Peas can be used in place of broad beans. Roasting lemons is one of the best techniques. The slightly charred slices hint at preserved lemons, though they are a little less intense.

Serves 4–6

255g freekeh
Fine sea salt and freshly
   ground black pepper
7 tablespoons extra virgin
   olive oil
450g asparagus, trimmed
1 lemon, rinsed and dried,
   end trimmed and cut
   crossways into
   3mm-thick rounds
1 large red onion, finely
   chopped
2 garlic cloves, thinly sliced
½ teaspoon fennel seeds,
   finely ground
250g shelled fresh broad
   beans (about 1kg in pods)
   or frozen broad beans,
   thawed
1–2 teaspoons Aleppo
   pepper or a pinch of
   cayenne pepper

1. Preheat the oven to 190°C/fan 170°C/gas mark 5. Line a rimmed tray with greaseproof paper.

2. In a large saucepan, combine 950ml of water, the freekeh, 1 teaspoon of salt and 1 tablespoon of oil. Bring to the boil over a high heat, then reduce to a gentle simmer, cover and cook for 40–45 minutes, until the freekeh is tender but still toothsome and the water is mostly absorbed.

3. Meanwhile, grill the asparagus for 10–12 minutes, depending on thickness, until crisp-tender. Transfer to a plate and, while hot, drizzle with 1 tablespoon of oil and season generously.

4. Lay the lemon slices in a single layer on the prepared baking tray, then drizzle with 2 tablespoons of oil and season with ¼ teaspoon each of salt and black pepper.

5. Roast the lemon slices for 18–24 minutes until golden, rotating the tray halfway through and transferring any quick-browning slices to a plate as they're ready. (Keep a careful eye on the slices; you want a nice golden colour.) Transfer the roasted slices to a plate to cool, then finely chop.

6. When the freekeh is ready, drain any excess water, then transfer to a large bowl.

7. Meanwhile, heat the remaining 3 tablespoons of oil in a large non-stick frying pan over a medium-high heat. Add the onion, garlic, fennel seeds and a generous pinch of salt. Reduce the heat to medium-low and gently cook for about

10 minutes, stirring occasionally, until the onion is tender. Add the chopped lemon and stir to combine. Cook for a further 2 minutes, then remove the pan from the heat.

8. Meanwhile, cook the broad beans in salted boiling water for 2 minutes. Drain and run under cold water to cool, then peel if using fresh beans. Add the beans and the onion mixture to the bowl with the freekeh. Cut the asparagus into 2.5cm lengths and add it as well.

9. Add ¼ teaspoon of salt and the Aleppo pepper or cayenne, then stir to combine. Adjust the seasoning to taste and serve.

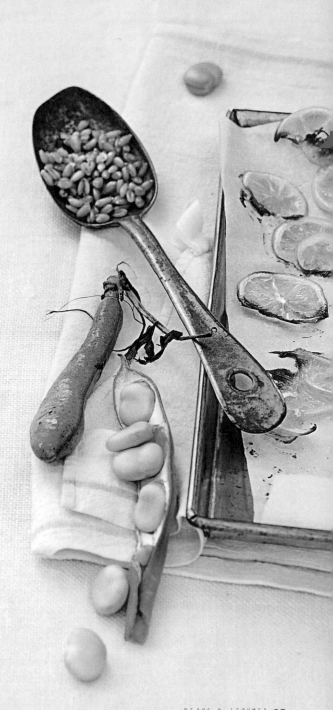

LEAFY
GREENS

JUICY CHICKEN WITH GARLIC SPINACH

*DAIRY-FREE

This slightly, or perhaps very, obscure way of cooking chicken breasts is based on the *recherché* restaurant technique of cooking *sous vide*. This is the rustic take on the method, which gives you an exceptionally tender and succulent interior without sacrificing the crisp outside.

Serves 4

Extra virgin olive oil
500g spinach, washed
  and dried
4 free-range chicken
  breasts, skin on
1.5 litres chicken or
  vegetable stock
Sea salt and freshly ground
  black pepper
3 garlic cloves, peeled
  and finely sliced
1–2 teaspoons finely
  sliced medium-hot
  red chilli
Lemon wedges, to serve

1. Heat a tablespoon of oil in a large frying pan, add a pile of spinach leaves (you will need to cook them in batches) and toss until they wilt. Remove them to a bowl and proceed with the remainder.

2. Lay the chicken breasts skin-side down on a board, flatten them with your hands, and cut out the white tendon from the underside if visible.

3. Bring the stock to the boil in a medium–large saucepan and season with salt. Turn the heat down as low as possible. Immerse the chicken breasts in the stock and cook for 15 minutes, without boiling. Transfer them to a plate and pat dry with kitchen paper. The stock can be used again: first pour it through a fine sieve, discarding any sediment in the base.

4. Heat ½ tablespoon of oil in a large frying pan over a medium heat, season the chicken breasts well and fry for several minutes on each side until golden. You may need to do this in batches, or use two pans.

5. Just before the chicken is ready, heat a tablespoon of oil in another frying pan over a medium heat, add the garlic and chilli and cook briefly until fragrant and lightly coloured, then stir in the spinach, season with salt and heat through. Serve the chicken and spinach accompanied by lemon wedges.

SPINACH TART

Spinach is one of the most tasty leafy greens, plus it's incredibly good for you – full of iron, vitamin A and antioxidants. Mixing it with cheese makes it doubly tasty. Use a prepared pastry case rather than making your own and it's doubly easy.

Serves 4

20cm deep tart tin, lined
   with shortcrust pastry or a
   ready-made pastry case
60g butter
300g spinach
1 onion, finely chopped
250g Cheddar, grated
2 medium eggs
2 medium egg yolks
200ml double cream
1 teaspoon French Dijon
   mustard
Salt and freshly
   ground black pepper

1. Preheat the oven to 200°C/ fan 180°C/gas mark 6. Place the pastry case in the oven and bake blind for 10–15 minutes.

2. Melt half the butter in a pan and gently cook the spinach until wilted. Remove from the pan and roughly chop. Heat the remaining butter and fry the onions until soft. Line the bottom of the pastry case with the spinach and onion.

3. Whisk together the cheese, eggs, egg yolks, cream, mustard and seasoning. Pour over the spinach and onion and bake in the oven for 20–30 minutes, until the top is golden. Turn off the heat and let the tart rest in the oven 5 minutes before serving.

GREEN DREAM
CLEANING MACHINE

*VEGETARIAN *DAIRY-FREE *GLUTEN-FREE

This juice is full of chlorophyll and rich in antioxidants, so important for cleansing and fighting damaging free radicals, but also very filling and nutritious. Swiss chard leaves contain at least 13 different antioxidants, plus a flavonoid called syringic acid, which has been shown to inhibit the activity of an enzyme that breaks down simple sugars, making this vegetable a great support for blood sugar control, very important when you are trying to control weight. Just look at these ingredients! You can't help but enjoy drinking this super-slimming green genie (pictured overleaf).

Serves 1

1 carrot
⅕ cucumber
A small bunch of parsley
A small handful of spinach
A small handful of Swiss
   chard
1 celery stick
1 lime

1. Juice all the ingredients, mix together and serve immediately.

Double up the quantities if you're serving to more than one person, but always make juice fresh to get the most out of your ingredients.

WATERCRESS WONDER

*VEGETARIAN *DAIRY FREE *GLUTEN FREE

Watercress is a fantastic ingredient for juicing, not only for its great flavour, but because it's rich in many vitamins – A (in the form of beta-carotene), C, E and K – and excellent in aiding calcium intake. Juiced with sulphur-rich asparagus, tart green apples, pineapple and cucumber it makes a light, fresh tangy juice. The bromelain contained in pineapple is an enzyme that assists in digestion by helping to break down proteins. This juice also makes a deliciously healthy appetiser. A truly delicious combo!

Serves 1

A large handful of watercress
4 asparagus spears
1 green apple
1 × 2cm thick slice fresh
   pineapple, skin removed
¼ cucumber

1. Juice all the ingredients, mix well and serve immediately.

Juicing is a fantastic way to extract nutrients from fresh fruits and vegetables, along with the water content, to produce a nutritionally rich and concentrated drink.

WARM CHICKEN & WATERCRESS

Pink grapefruit is an underused ingredient but its interesting sweet/sour flavour works well with chicken. The marinated red onion is key and makes this a really memorable dish with great flavour and texture.

Serves 2 as a main course or 4 as a starter

1 large red onion, very thinly sliced
150ml white wine vinegar
100g granulated sugar
2 Little Gem lettuces
60g watercress
1 tablespoon olive oil
200g cooked chicken, roughly shredded
1 pink grapefruit, peel and pith removed, cut into segments

For the dressing
2 tablespoons extra virgin olive oil
2 teaspoons white wine vinegar
1 heaped teaspoon grainy mustard
1 teaspoon honey

1. Place the sliced red onion in a small heatproof bowl. Put the white wine vinegar and sugar in a small pan and heat gently, stirring occasionally, until the sugar dissolves. Increase the heat and bring to the boil. Pour the sweetened vinegar over the onions and leave to marinate for 10 minutes–1 hour.

2. Separate the lettuce leaves and place in a large bowl with the watercress. Combine the dressing ingredients in a screw-top jar, shake well then pour over the leaves and toss well to combine.

3. Then, in a non-stick pan, heat a tablespoon of olive oil until very hot. Add the shredded chicken meat to the pan, leave for 2 minutes until starting to crisp up, then turn once or twice until it is golden and crispy.

4. On a serving dish, arrange the dressed leaves, grapefruit segments and crispy chicken and top with the drained marinated onions.

This salad would be a good way to use up leftover Christmas turkey instead of chicken.

LEEK, WATERCRESS & CHEESE VICHYSOISSE

This is one the best chilled soups. The cheese adds a little tanginess which blends well with the leek and peppery watercress.

Serves 4

1 onion, chopped
3 leeks, chopped
50g unsalted butter
225g new potatoes, chopped
900ml vegetable or chicken stock
100g bunch of watercress
5 tablespoons single cream
90ml milk
75g Roquefort cheese, crumbled
Salt and freshly ground black pepper

1. Sweat the onion and leeks in the butter for about 5 minutes, until beginning to wilt. Add the potatoes and cook for 5 minutes longer.

2. Add the stock and bring to the boil, then reduce the heat to a simmer and cook for 25 minutes, until all the vegetables are soft.

3. Remove from the heat. Add the leaves from the bunch of watercress and leave to infuse in the pan for 5 minutes, then blitz to a smooth purée in a blender.

4. Put the cream, milk and Roquefort in a small pan and heat gently, stirring until smooth. Add to the soup, stir well together and add seasoning. Strain through a fine sieve, then chill until ready to serve.

WATERCRESS & SALMON SALAD

*GLUTEN-FREE *DAIRY-FREE

Combining salmon with the peppery taste of watercress makes a very tasty and satisfying meal. Fresh or canned salmon can be used as both are rich in long-chain omega-3 fats.

Serves 2

150g baby new potatoes
   (2–3 per person)
80g broccoli
80g watercress, washed
   and dried
2 cooked salmon fillets,
   flaked, or 200g canned
   salmon

For the dressing
3 tablespoons olive oil
1 tablespoon lemon juice
1 teaspoon mustard
1 tablespoon chopped
   fresh dill
1 teaspoon honey

1. Whisk together all the dressing ingredients until well combined and set aside.

2. Boil the baby potatoes for about 10 minutes or until just cooked, adding the broccoli for the last 1–2 minutes (you want it just tender, not overcooked). Drain and when cool enough to handle, slice the potatoes.

3. To assemble, place the watercress in a serving dish, add the salmon, potatoes and broccoli and drizzle with the dressing.

Use asparagus, when in season, to replace or complement the broccoli.

SALMON RAVIOLI & WATERCRESS PESTO

The smokey flavours of the salmon, the creaminess of the goat's cheese and the pesto make a delicious combination, and using the delicious Fresh Dillisk Pasta on page 52 to create the ravioli takes this dish to the next level.

Serves 6

1 quantity Fresh Dillisk
  Pasta (see overleaf)
150g soft goat's cheese
150g smoked salmon,
  cut into pieces
Sea salt and freshly
  ground black pepper

For the watercress pesto
110g fresh watercress
150ml extra virgin olive oil
25g pine kernels, toasted
2 garlic cloves, peeled
50g Parmesan cheese, grated

1. Cut the dillisk pasta into strips about 10cm wide and place teaspoonfuls of goat's cheese at 7.5cm intervals down the strip. Season the smoked salmon with salt and pepper and place a teaspoon of it on top of each piece of cheese.

2. Fold the pasta over the filling and press down around it to seal it in. Cut out the pasta parcels with a sharp knife and crimp the edges with a fork to ensure that the filling doesn't ooze out during cooking.

3. Put a large saucepan of salted water over a high heat and bring to the boil. Drop in the ravioli and cook for 5 minutes.

4. While the pasta is cooking, make the watercress pesto. Put the watercress, oil, pine kernels, garlic and grated cheese in a food processor and blend for a couple of minutes.

5. Drain the ravioli from the water, and return to the saucepan. Pour the watercress pesto on top and toss gently.

6. Season with pepper and serve.

FRESH DILLISK PASTA *VEGETARIAN *DAIRY-FREE

The coast has an abundance of fantastic seaweed and over the past ten years it has started to make its way back on to menus across the country. Dillisk, also known as dulce, is a red alga that holds a subtle flavour of the sea and marries well with fresh pasta.

Makes approx. 1kg

500g durum pasta flour, plus extra for dusting
4 tablespoons dried dillisk, finely chopped
Large pinch of sea salt
7 medium eggs
Semolina flour, for dusting

1. Place the flour, dillisk, salt and eggs in a food processor and blend together until a dough forms. Place the dough on a floured board and knead until smooth. Separate the dough into 6 balls, cover with a tea towel and allow to rest in a cool place or in the fridge for 30 minutes.

2. If you have a pasta machine, set it up and push the dough through the rollers 8 times. With each pass through the rollers, reduce the setting, until you reach the final setting. Be careful that the pasta does not break as you should now have a long, thin sheet. If you don't have a pasta maker, roll the dough out very thinly with a rolling pin. (This can be hard as it breaks easily – buy a pasta maker; they are inexpensive and so useful.)

3. Then, dust the pasta sheet lightly with semolina flour and hang over a clean clothes horse or similar for 10 minutes. Store in the fridge, and eat within 2 days.

CAESAR SALAD *VEGETARIAN

This book could not be complete without this classic lettuce salad. The Cos lettuce is jam-packed with vitamin A, but the olive oil, used on the croutons and in the dressing, is also very nutritious. It contains healthy fats and antioxidants, so it is well worth purchasing good-quality oil.

Serves 2

½ small ciabatta, cut
   into large cubes
Olive oil
Salt and freshly ground
   black pepper
1 large egg
1 garlic clove, crushed
1 tablespoon lime juice
1 teaspoon vegetarian
   Worcestershire sauce
1 teaspoon Dijon mustard
1 Cos or Romaine lettuce, torn
   or roughly chopped
25g vegetarian Parmesan,
   grated

1. Preheat the oven to 190°C/ fan 170°C/gas mark 5. To make the croûtons, toss the ciabatta in 1 tablespoon of oil and season well. Spread on a baking tray and cook until crisp and golden, about 10 minutes.

2. Place the egg in a pan, cover with cold water and bring to the boil. Boil for 1 minute then transfer the egg to a bowl of cold water to stop it cooking. Once it is cool enough to handle, crack the egg into a food-processor and add the garlic, lime juice, Worcestershire sauce, mustard and 2½ tablespoons of oil. Process well, then season with salt and freshly ground black pepper to taste.

3. To serve, place the lettuce in a large serving bowl, pour over the dressing and top with the croûtons and Parmesan. Toss well and serve straight away.

GRILLED SARDINES & LAMB'S LETTUCE

*GLUTEN-FREE *DAIRY-FREE

This simple salad defies seasons – it makes a fitting lunch on a hot summer's afternoon, a nice starter for a winter festive meal or a nutrient-packed any-time dish. Serve it family-style from a large platter or as individual servings on pretty plates.

Serves 4

1 medium fennel bulb, including stems and fronds
8 fresh sardines, cleaned, leaving head and tail intact
2 lemons
3 tablespoons extra virgin olive oil, plus more for brushing
½ teaspoon Aleppo pepper or pinch cayenne
Fine sea salt and freshly ground black pepper
115g lamb's lettuce

1. Finely chop half the fennel, including half the fronds.

2. Rinse the sardines and pat dry, then spread out on a platter. Finely zest 1 lemon over the top, turning the sardines to cover both sides. Drizzle with ½ tablespoon of the oil and sprinkle the outside and cavities with the fennel stems, Aleppo pepper and a generous ¼ teaspoon of salt.

3. Squeeze 2 teaspoons of lemon juice into a small bowl and set aside. Cut the remaining whole lemon crossways into 3mm-thick rounds. Discard the seeds.

4. Heat a barbecue or a griddle pan until hot. Brush with oil and grill the sardines, in batches if needed, for 4–5 minutes per batch, turning once until just cooked through. Using a metal spatula, transfer the cooked fish to a clean large plate.

5. Lightly season the lemon slices with salt and black pepper, then grill for about 1 minute on each side until lightly charred. Transfer to a large bowl.

6. Thinly shave the remaining half fennel bulb and place in the bowl with the lemon. Add the reserved lemon juice, the remaining 2½ tablespoons of oil, half the fennel fronds, ½ teaspoon salt and a generous pinch of black pepper; toss to combine. Add the lamb's lettuce and very gently toss to combine.

7. Divide the salad and the sardines between four serving plates and garnish with the remaining fennel fronds.

If cooking on a barbecue, use a grill tray to prevent the lemon slices from slipping into the coals. If you can't find lamb's lettuce, any small tender lettuce will do.

FATTOUSH SALAD WITH RADISH

*VEGETARIAN *DAIRY-FREE

Fattoush is an eastern bread salad made with toasted pitta and fresh vegetables. Once all the vegetables have been sliced it's super quick to put together – perfect for a relaxed summer lunch. Plus it's bolstered by vitamins A and K from the Little Gem lettuces, to help protect and heal skin.

Serves 4

1 cucumber, peeled, deseeded and cut into 1cm dice
3 pitta breads
2 cloves garlic, crushed
Juice of 1 lemon
3 tablespoons extra virgin olive oil
2 Little Gem lettuces, roughly chopped
6 radishes, sliced
1 red onion, finely chopped
5 ripe tomatoes, peeled, deseeded and roughly chopped
4 tablespoons roughly chopped purslane leaves
2 tablespoons each roughly chopped flat-leaf parsley, coriander leaves and mint
Salt and freshly ground black pepper

1. Place the diced cucumber in a colander, sprinkle with salt and leave to drain for 20 minutes.

2. Meanwhile, toast the pitta bread, then cut into small strips

3. In a large bowl, mix together the garlic, lemon juice and olive oil to make a dressing.

4. Wipe off any excess salt from the cucumber and add to the bowl along with the diced vegetables, herbs and pitta and toss well to coat with the dressing. Season with salt and pepper and serve straight away.

ROCKET, RASPBERRY & GORGONZOLA

They serve something similar to this salad in the beautiful Olympic café in Kalk Bay, which sells some of the best coffee in South Africa. They don't bother with the usual formal café rules, and operate as a hotch-potch of rustic charm and enviable style.

Serves 4

2 tablespoons olive oil
2 big chunks of brown
  bread, cut into croûtons
½ teaspoon salt
200g raspberries, the
  plumpest you can find
70g wild rocket
150g Gorgonzola, pulled
  into chunks

For the dressing
2 tablespoons raspberry
  vinegar
1 teaspoon Dijon mustard
2 tablespoons extra virgin
  olive oil

1. You need to make the croûtons first so they aren't too hot when they hit the salad leaves. Heat the oil in a medium frying pan and when the oil is sparking a little, add the bread. When the croûtons are in the pan, throw over a little salt and fry until they all have a crunch. Keep tossing the pan so one side doesn't colour more than the other.

2. To make the dressing, put all the ingredients in a jug and mix as thoroughly as you can – do this without the dressing jumping out of the jug and staining your shirt!

3. Combine the raspberries, rocket and Gorgonzola in a bowl and pour over the dressing. Toss together (gently so you don't bruise any of those rocket leaves) and add the croûtons. Serve in a big pile on an even bigger plate.

Try to find raspberry vinegar for the dressing – it's a valuable ingredient to have in your store cupboard – but if you find it hard to come by use white wine vinegar instead. If you're a vegetarian, use a vegetarian alternative to gorgonzola, such as dolcelatte.

BUTTERNUT SQUASH & ROCKET SALAD

*VEGETARIAN *GLUTEN-FREE *DAIRY-FREE

This is a great low-carb lunch and is Paleo-friendly. Butternut squash is the perfect vegetable replacement to satisfy all your carb cravings.

Serves 4

1 large butternut squash, peeled and halved (seeds discarded)
2 tablespoons olive oil
1 tablespoon chopped thyme
1 tablespoon raw honey, melted
225g rocket leaves
120g toasted pumpkin seeds
Freshly ground black pepper

For the dressing
4 tablespoons olive oil
Juice of ½ lemon
Juice of ½ orange
1 teaspoon Dijon mustard
1 teaspoon chopped thyme leaves

1. Preheat the oven to 220°C/fan 200°C/gas mark 7.

2. Chop the butternut squash into wedges and place in a large bowl. Drizzle over the oil, add the thyme and toss to coat. Place on a baking tray and cook in the oven for 30 minutes. Every 10 minutes, remove the baking tray and toss the squash so that all the edges become roasted and caramelised.

3. After 30 minutes, toss one last time, drizzle with the honey, cook for a further 5 minutes, then set aside to cool slightly.

4. Meanwhile, mix all the dressing ingredients together and dress the rocket leaves in a large bowl. Scatter the pumpkin seeds on top and toss with the butternut squash. Finish with a few grinds of black pepper and serve.

Butternut squash has a lovely sweet, nutty taste so you don't have to do much to it. it's lovely to eat raw, but it's really perfect roasted, when it caramelises beautifully.

SWISS CHARD, ALLSPICE & POMEGRANATE

*VEGETARIAN *DAIRY-FREE *GLUTEN-FREE

Like so many cabbages, Swiss chard greets spices and fruits like old friends – they get on very well together, and any potential austerity is further softened by a mass of golden fried onions and a generous addition of coriander.

Serves 6

3 tablespoons extra
  virgin olive oil
2 large onions, peeled, halved
  and finely sliced across
A slug of vinegar, (white
  wine or cider)
500–600g Swiss chard
½ teaspoon allspice
Sea salt
30g coriander leaves,
  roughly chopped
Sumac (optional)
3 heaped tablespoons
  pomegranate seeds

1. Heat 2 tablespoons of oil in a large saucepan over a medium heat and fry the onions for 15–20 minutes, stirring frequently, until creamy and golden.

2. At the same time bring a large saucepan of water to the boil and acidulate it with a slug of vinegar. Cut the chard leaves off the stalks and thickly slice them, then thinly slice the stalks. Add the stalks to the pan and cook for 5 minutes, then add the leaves and cook for a further 2 minutes. Drain into a colander and shake dry.

3. Stir the allspice into the onions, and then add the chard. Season with salt and gently fry for a couple of minutes to acquaint the ingredients, then stir in the coriander. Transfer to a serving dish, drizzle over the remaining tablespoon of oil, scatter over some sumac if wished and then the pomegranate seeds.

BRASSICAS

KALE CRISPS

*VEGETARIAN *GLUTEN-FREE *DAIRY-FREE

Kale is all over the place, on restaurant menus, at farmers' markets, on supermarket shelves, and kale crisps are the snack of the moment. It's super nutritious – curly kale works best for this recipe.

Makes lots

250g curly kale
2 tablespoons extra
   virgin olive oil
Sea salt
Sugar

1. Preheat the oven to 150°C/fan 130°C/gas mark 2. Strip the leaves off the kale, tear into bite-sized pieces and put in a bowl. Sprinkle with extra virgin olive oil, a little salt and a pinch of sugar and toss well. Spread out in a single layer on two baking trays.

2. Bake in the preheated oven for approx. 20 minutes until crisp. Transfer to a wire rack to cool and crisp further. Enjoy.

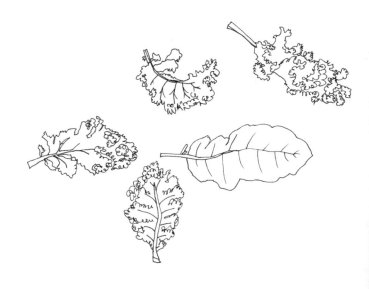

WILD RICE, KALE & POMEGRANATE

*VEGETARIAN *GLUTEN-FREE *DAIRY-FREE

This hearty salad is a very modern recipe that is packed with super foods and classic Turkish ingredients. The combination of the mixed rice – using black, red, brown and white – gives the salad a variety of colours, textures and flavours. Turkish staples dill, parsley, mint, pomegranate seeds and walnuts add flavour, and the addition of kale gives it a light, modern twist. The dressing uses sumac to give an extra sour note. A little pinch of this ground red berry is a lovely way to introduce more depth of flavour to any salad dressing.

Serves 4–6

350g mix of black, red, brown and white rice
150g kale
A handful of finely chopped dill
2 handfuls of finely chopped flat-leaf parsley leaves
A handful of finely chopped mint leaves
1 red chilli, deseeded and finely chopped
200g pomegranate seeds
55g walnuts, lightly crushed

For the dressing
4 tablespoons olive oil
3 tablespoons pomegranate molasses
Juice of 1 lemon
1 teaspoon caster sugar
1 teaspoon of sumac
Sea salt and freshly ground black pepper

1. Cook the rice in a large pan of boiling water according to packet instructions, starting with the variety that takes the longest and adding the rest at appropriate times so that they all cook perfectly. Drain and rinse under cold running water. Set aside to drain.

2. Meanwhile, cook the kale for 2–3 minutes in a large pan of boiling water. Drain and refresh under cold running water. When cold, drain thoroughly and squeeze out the excess water with your hands.

3. Whisk all the dressing ingredients together in a small bowl.

4. Put the drained rice in a large mixing bowl and add the kale, herbs, chilli and half the pomegranate seeds and walnuts. Pour in three-quarters of the dressing and mix everything together thoroughly.

5. Tip the salad onto a serving dish and pour over the remaining dressing. Top with the remaining pomegranate seeds and walnuts and serve immediately.

SPROUTING GREENS JUICE

This is a seriously green juice – in colour and taste. If you choose only one skin-saving juice, make it this one! Kale is a true skin super food, not only rich in vitamin K, but also highly prized amongst nutritionists for its omega-3 content and over 40 different flavonoids that make it both an antioxidant and anti-inflammatory. Broccoli sprouts have been shown to contain levels of sulforaphane 100 times higher than those found in the plant itself. Sulforaphane is a compound that improves the liver's ability to detoxify, an essential process for skin clarity and overall health.

Serves 4

4–5 handfuls of kale
A handful of parsley
2 kiwi fruit, peeled
1 lime
A handful of broccoli
    sprouts
½ teaspoon spirulina

1. Juice all the fruit, vegetables and sprouts, and then stir in the spirulina before serving.

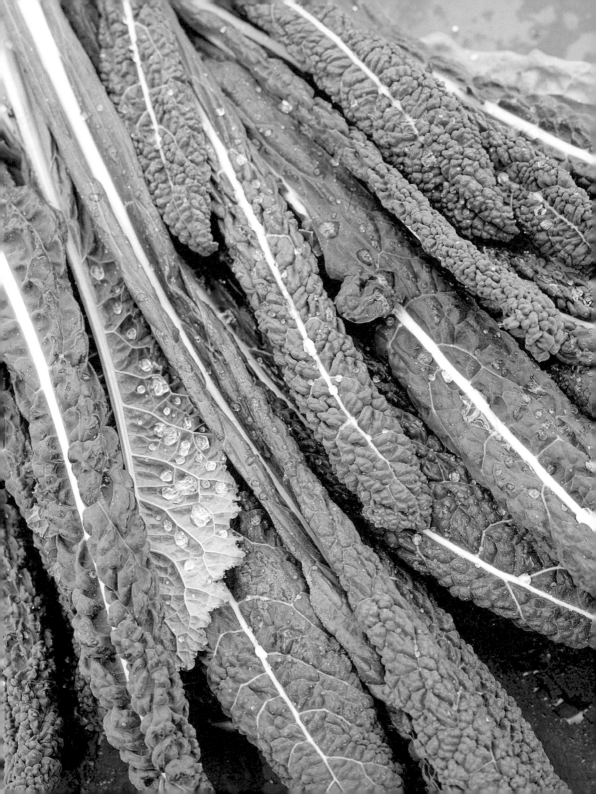

PAPPARDELLE WITH CAVOLO NERO *VEGETARIAN

Cavolo nero – kale's Italian cousin, also known as black kale – is a nutrition powerhouse and combining it with heart-healthy garlic makes this dish extra good for you. You can swap the crème fraîche for yogurt for an extra health-boost, but watch the sauce carefully as it can easily split.

Serves 4

200g pappardelle
2 tablespoons olive oil
4 garlic cloves, finely
   chopped
200g cavolo nero, stalks
   removed, roughly chopped
Sea salt and freshly ground
   black pepper
150ml white wine
4 tablespoons crème fraîche
4 tablespoons freshly
   grated vegetarian
   Parmesan, plus extra
   to serve

1. Bring a large saucepan of salted water to the boil. Add the pappardelle and cook for 6–8 minutes, until al dente.

2. Meanwhile, heat the olive oil in a medium saucepan, then add the chopped garlic. Add the cavolo and stir to wilt in the oil. Season with salt and pepper. Pour in the white wine and boil for 3–5 minutes until reduced.

3. Stir in the crème fraîche and Parmesan. Drain the pasta, mix with the sauce and serve straight away with some extra Parmesan sprinkled on top.

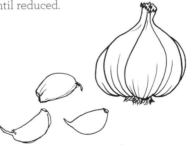

CAVOLO NERO WITH SOBA NOODLES *VEGETARIAN *DAIRY-FR

Delicate and beautiful, these noodles are tossed with a sweet ginger dressing and pepped with lime. There is plenty of blanched cavolo nero and bright avocado for good measure. Try eating this with extra soy for a salty edge.

Serves 4

250g soba noodles
1 head of cavolo nero
   (about 200g)
1 ripe avocado
4 spring onions, sliced
40g sesame seeds,
   to garnish

For the dressing
1–2 garlic cloves, crushed
1 teaspoon tamarind paste
4cm piece of root ginger,
   peeled and finely grated
1 tablespoon maple syrup
2 tablespoons extra virgin
   olive oil
2 teaspoons sesame oil
Finely grated zest and juice
   of 1 unwaxed lime

1. Cook the soba noodles by adding them to boiling water and simmering, according to the pack instructions, usually for about 5 minutes. Drain and rinse well under running water until cool.

2. Meanwhile, separate the cavolo nero leaves and then trim the tough base of each. Roughly chop them and cook in a pan of lightly salted boiling water for 3-4 minutes, until tender. Cool and drain well then squeeze out any excess water and roughly chop.

3. Make the dressing by putting all the ingredients (including any ginger juice) into a jar and mix well until combined.

4. Cut the avocado flesh into 2cm chunks and set aside.

5. Put the noodles and cavolo nero into a large bowl and pour over the dressing. Combine thoroughly before carefully mixing through the avocado and spring onion; a light touch will mean the avocado doesn't turn to mush.

6. Serve on plates sprinkled with sesame seeds.

BRAISED CAVOLO NERO *VEGETARIAN

Crinkled black kale is known as cavolo nero (black Tuscan cabbage). Serve it on its own, as a vegetable or as a topping for polenta.

Serves 4–6

4 heads cavolo nero
Sea salt and freshly
   ground black pepper
3 tablespoons extra
   virgin olive oil
2 garlic cloves, peeled
   and finely sliced
Extra virgin olive oil
Bruchetta, toasted

1. Remove the stems from the cavolo nero leaves. Blanch in a large pot of boiling, well-salted water for 3–5 minutes. Be careful not to overcook. Drain well.

2. Heat the olive oil in a heavy-based saucepan. Add the garlic and fry gently. When it begins to colour, add the cavolo nero and season generously with salt and pepper.

3. Cook for about 5 minutes. Transfer to a bowl and drizzle generously with extra virgin olive oil.

4. Serve on top of grilled or toasted bruschetta.

QUINOA CABBAGE ROLLS

Try varying this recipe by adding some nuts, or serve the quinoa as a dish on its own sprinkled with gruyère. Try substituting the cabbage with chard leaves.

Serves 4

10g dried cèpes
4 tablespoons olive oil
1 onion, finely chopped
2 sticks celery, finely chopped
2 carrots, finely chopped
3 garlic cloves, finely chopped
100g chestnut mushrooms, finely sliced
100g quinoa
200ml red wine
Sea salt and freshly ground black pepper
80g cooked chickpeas
1 large cabbage, such as Savoy
2 × 400g cans tomatoes, crushed
1 teaspoon sugar
Pinch of sea salt
100g grated gruyère

1. Preheat the oven to 180°C/fan 160°C/gas mark 4.

2. Cover the cèpes with 300ml of boiling water and leave to soak. Meanwhile, heat half the oil in a medium-sized saucepan. Add half of the onion, celery, carrots and garlic and cook over a medium heat until softened. Add the chestnut mushrooms and cook for a further 3 minutes.

3. Add the quinoa and cook for a minute, stirring all the time. Pour in the soaked cèpes and their liquid, add half the wine and season generously. Bring to the boil, reduce the heat to a simmer, cover and cook for approximately 15–20 minutes until tender and most of the liquid has been absorbed. Once cooked, season as necessary and stir in the chickpeas.

4. Bring a large pan of salted water to the boil. Using a small knife, carefully remove the core from the cabbage, peel away 8–12 leaves and cook in the boiling water for 5 minutes or until softened. Drain and run under cold water to refresh, then drain again.

5. Remove the tough centre stalks and lay the leaves on a work surface, vein side down. Place approximately 2 heaped tablespoons of quinoa mix on one half of the leaf, and roll up, folding the sides in to form a parcel. The size of the leaves will differ so fill and wrap accordingly. Place in a large ovenproof dish, seam side down.

6. Heat the remaining oil over a medium heat, add the remaining onion, celery, carrots and garlic and cook until softened. Add the remaining wine and tomatoes, sugar and salt and bring to the boil. Reduce the heat and simmer until reduced by half. Pour over the cabbage leaves, cover with foil and cook in the oven until tender, approximately 40 minutes.

7. Serve hot, sprinkled with gruyère cheese.

CABBAGE & HONEY SALMON *DAIRY-FREE *GLUTEN-FREE

Honey and ginger are two amazing ingredients as they create magic when cooked together. Both are also excellent for the immune system so this makes a lovely dinner all through the winter months.

Serves 4

4 × 300g skinless salmon
   fillets

For the glaze
2 tablespoons raw honey
1 tablespoon Dijon mustard
Juice of 1 lemon
2.5cm piece of root ginger,
   peeled and grated

For the cabbage
3 tablespoons olive oil
1 small cabbage, sliced
   into thin strips
1 garlic clove, crushed
1 tablespoon sesame seeds,
   plus extra to garnish
Freshly ground black
   pepper
4 spring onions, chopped

1. Heat a large, non-stick pan over a high heat and add the salmon – if you have a good-quality, non-stick pan, there should be enough oils in the salmon to cook it without the need to add any extra oil. Cook the salmon for 3–4 minutes on each side.

2. Meanwhile, make the glaze. Place the honey, mustard, lemon and ginger together in a bowl and stir to combine. Set aside.

3. When your salmon is just about cooked, spoon the glaze over the top, then take off the heat. The glaze will caramelise in the hot pan and turn the salmon sticky and brown.

4. To cook the cabbage, heat half the olive oil in a wok over a medium heat. Add the cabbage and stir fry for 3–4 minutes, then add the remaining oil and cook for another 5 minutes, tossing all the time (if you need more moisture, add a drop or two of water). Add the garlic and sesame seeds and cook for a further minute.

5. Turn the cabbage out onto a plate, season with black pepper and top with the glazed salmon. Scatter the spring onion over the top and serve with a few extra sesame seeds.

WOK-FRIED CHOI SUM WITH SHIITAKE

Oriental-style greens are much more commonplace than they used to be, thanks to the growth of interest in Thai and Chinese cooking. All the ingredients for this dish are readily available – so get to wok!

Serves 4

450g choi sum
2 tablespoons groundnut oil
1 garlic clove, crushed
1 tablespoon finely
   chopped fresh ginger
100g shiitake mushrooms
75g fresh or canned Chinese
   water chestnuts, peeled
   and thinly sliced
100ml chicken stock
2 tablespoons cornflour
2 tablespoons tamari
1 tablespoon sesame oil
1 tablespoon roasted peanuts

1. Separate the stems from the leaves of the choi sum and cut them into 5cm long pieces. Blanch the stems in boiling salted water until just tender, then drain well.

2. Heat a wok or deep frying pan, add the groundnut oil, garlic, ginger, choi sum stems, mushrooms and water chestnuts and stir-fry for 3–4 minutes. Add the choi sum leaves and cook for a minute longer.

3. Blend the stock with the cornflour to form a paste and stir it into the pan. Stir in the tamari and sesame oil and toss well together. The sauce should form a glaze around the vegetables. Sprinkle over the peanuts and serve immediately.

PORK ROAST WITH BROCCOLI RABE

*GLUTEN-FREE

Pork and seafood is a great combination as their flavours augment each other. Here, they are used in a dish straddling the French–Chinese cuisine line. Young green garlic and *gai lan*, or Chinese broccoli, are stewed in butter and finished with tender bay scallops. Fermented black beans add a subtle umami layer that ties the dish together. The combination of flavours is like a symphony. It is stunning.

Serves 4

50g fermented black beans
Pinch of ground clove
Pinch of ground cardamom
1 teaspoon ground coriander
1 tablespoon chopped
    young garlic, plus
    60g thinly sliced
900g pork loin
Sea salt and freshly ground
    black pepper
240g gai lan or broccoli rabe
1 tablespoon julienned
    fresh ginger
60g unsalted butter,
    softened
225g bay scallops, rinsed
Rice wine vinegar

1. In a small pot over a high heat, combine 120ml water with the black beans, spices and chopped garlic. Boil until reduced by three-quarters. Transfer to a blender and purée until smooth. Set aside.

2. Season the pork with salt and pepper. In a large frying pan over a high heat, sauté the pork loin, fat side down, until browned and crisp, or about 7 minutes.

3. Drain the rendered fat from the pan and save for another use. Turn the pork over and cook until browned, or about 10 minutes more.

4. Reduce the temperature to low and cook until the interior of the loin is cooked but still rosy, or about 5 minutes more. Transfer to a clean platter to rest for 10 minutes.

5. Return the frying pan with the pan drippings to the heat and add the gai lan, sliced garlic and ginger. Cook until the gai lan begins to wilt, then add the butter and cook for 1 minute more.

6. Remove the pan from the heat and add the scallops. Season with salt and vinegar. The scallops will warm through as the pan cools.

7. Thinly slice the pork across and divide between four dinner plates. Top with the black bean purée and serve with the gai lan mixture. Serve immediately.

STIR-FRY WITH SPRING VEG *VEGETARIAN

Crisp fresh broad beans and broccoli are good sources of fibre – pair them with pak choi and you have a quick and delicious meal providing vitamins A and C as well as potassium.

Serves 4

200g noodles of your choice
1 tablespoon vegetable oil
250g purple sprouting or
   tenderstem broccoli, cut
   into small florets
4 garlic cloves, finely chopped
1cm piece root ginger,
   finely chopped
1 red chilli, deseeded and
   finely sliced
A bunch of spring onions,
   sliced
150g broad beans
   (600g unshelled weight),
   cooked and peeled of
   outer skins if large
2 heads pak choi, thickly
   sliced
1½ tablespoons hoisin sauce
1 tablespoon soy sauce

1. Bring a large saucepan of water to the boil and cook the noodles according to the packet instructions, or until just tender. Drain well and rinse with cold water to stop them cooking further.

2. Heat the oil in a non-stick wok or frying pan. Add the broccoli, then fry on a high heat for 5 minutes or until just tender, adding a little water if it begins to catch. Add the garlic, ginger and chilli, fry for a further minute, then toss through the spring onions, broad beans and pak choi. Stir-fry for 2–3 minutes.

3. Add the hoisin and soy sauces and warm through. Toss the noodles in with the vegetables to warm and serve.

ROASTED BROCCOLI WITH BULGAR *VEGETARIAN

Broccoli should be given more attention. Florets are so often forced to sit on the side of a plate, lacking lustre and boiled beyond recognition, but this should not be their destiny. With careful cooking and a few sophisticated ingredients – tart dried cherries, bulgar wheat and pistachio nuts – the broccoli steps up and tastes unrecognisably chic.

Serves 3

1 healthy-size head of broccoli, divided into florets
2 tablespoons olive oil
150g bulgar wheat
50g dried cherries, plus a few to garnish
50g pistachios, roughly chopped
Zest of 1 unwaxed lemon

For the dressing
3 tablespoons Greek yogurt
2 tablespoons red wine vinegar
1 tablespoon extra virgin olive oil
Sea salt and freshly ground black pepper

1. Preheat the oven to 180°C/ fan 160°C/gas mark 4. Spread the broccoli florets out on a tray and drizzle them well with olive oil. Put them in the oven to roast for 20 minutes.

2. Meanwhile make your bulgar wheat by tipping it into a large bowl and seasoning. Pour over 150ml boiling water. Cover the bowl with clingfilm and allow it to sit for 10 minutes. Remove the clingfilm, fluff the bulgar wheat up with a fork and stir through the dried cherries, pistachios, lemon zest and roasted broccoli.

3. To make the dressing, mix all the dressing ingredients together with a dash of hot water. Pour the dressing over the salad and gently toss until well combined. Serve in one, two or three bowls garnished with a few extra dried cherries. Serve immediately.

BUTTON SPROUTS
WITH PARMESAN

At Christmas, Brussels sprouts cooking in boiling water and tossed with butter are enjoyable enough but rather uninspiring. This recipe is a more interesting way to prepare them, combining tiny Brussels with sweet onions and a dusting of fresh Parmesan.

Serves 4 as a side

3 tablespoons olive oil
20 small pearl onions,
    blanched and peeled
1 tablespoon light
    muscovado sugar
40g unsalted butter
200ml meat stock
350g button sprouts
    (baby Brussels sprouts)
2 tablespoons freshly
    grated Parmesan cheese
Salt and freshly ground
    black pepper

1. Heat the oil in a frying pan in which the onions will fit in a single layer, add the onions and cook over a high heat until golden all over. Add the sugar and half the butter and cook until the onions are caramelised, about 8–10 minutes. Pour in the stock and cook until it has evaporated.

2. Meanwhile, cook the Brussels sprouts in boiling salted water until just tender but still retaining a little bite. Drain them well.

3. In a separate pan, heat the remaining butter until foaming, add the sprouts and sauté for 5 minutes, until golden. Add the onions and toss together, then season with salt and pepper and transfer to a serving dish. Sprinkle with the Parmesan and toss to coat.

Brussels sprouts are a strange vegetable, inspiring either love or hate. Here are some great ways to serve them:
• Tossed with the roasted chestnuts and celery
• Puréed and finish simply with nutmeg and butter
• Mixed with cream and seasoned with a little curry powder

SHAVED BRUSSELS
SPROUTS *GLUTEN-FREE

Very thinly sliced raw Brussels sprouts tossed with lots of good-quality extra virgin olive oil, zingy lemon juice and peppery, slightly tart aged sheeps' cheese is enough to convert even the most ardent sprout-adverse folk. Try it when Brussels sprouts are in season, from late August to March, and see for yourself. This salad loses its lemony punch if it sits for too long, so serve immediately.

Serves 4–6

450g Brussels sprouts
5 tablespoons good-quality
  extra virgin olive oil
½ teaspoon fine sea salt
3½ tablespoons fresh
  lemon juice
½ teaspoon whole black
  peppercorns, crushed
115g semi-soft pecorino
  cheese studded with
  black peppercorns,
  very thinly shaved

1. Rinse the Brussels sprouts, then pat dry with kitchen paper. Remove any outer leaves that have brown spots or have yellowed, then cut the sprouts in half, lengthwise. Very thinly slice the sprouts crosswise, transferring the sliced pieces to a large shallow serving bowl as you go. Discard the stems.

2. Drizzle the oil over the sprouts, then sprinkle with the salt and toss well to combine. Add the lemon juice, then the crushed pepper and toss once more. Lay the cheese over the top of the salad and serve immediately.

In speciality cheese shops and delicatessens, you may find semi-soft pecorino cheese studded with black peppercorns; it will often be labelled rustico. If you can't find one with peppercorns, add more crushed peppercorns to this dish.

INDEX

ACKNOWLEDGEMENTS

The publishers would like to thank the following for kind permission to reproduce their recipes:

Eric Skokan © pp12, 84 from *Farm Fork Food*

Rachel DeThample © pp15, 16 from *Less Meat More Veg*

Paul Gayler © pp19, 27 from *Pure Vegetarian*; pp23, 47, 83, 91 from *Passion for Veg*

Jimmy Garcia © p20 from *Social Eats*

Margaret Rayman © pp24, 44, 49 from *Healthy Eating to Reduce the Risk of Dementia*

Mindy Fox © pp28, 34–35, 54, 93 from *Perfectly Tossed Salad*

Annie Rigg © p30 from *Summer Berries & Autumn Fruit*

Darina Allen © pp33, 67 from *30 Years at Ballymaloe*; p77 from *Forgotten Skills of Cooking*

Annie Bell © pp38, 62 from *Low Carb Revolution*

Liz Earle © pp41, 43, 71 from *Juice*

Clodagh McKenna © pp50–52 from *Clodagh's Irish Kitchen*

Georgina Fuggle © pp58, 74, 88 from *Take One Veg*

Dan Green © pp61, 80 from *The Paleo Diet*

John Gregory-Smith © p68 from *Turkish Delights*

Maria Elia © p79 from *The Modern Vegetarian*

First published in Great Britain in 2016 by
Kyle Books, an imprint of Kyle Cathie Ltd
192–198 Vauxhall Bridge Road
London SW1V 1DX
general.enquiries@kylebooks.com
www.kylebooks.co.uk

10 9 8 7 6 5 4 3 2 1

ISBN 978 0 85783 384 6

Text © see page 95
Design © 2016 Kyle Books
Illustrations © 2016 Jenni Desmond
Photographs © see below

Pages 2, 22, 29, 34–35, 55, 93 © Ellen
Silverman; 4 (left), 8, 32, 66 © Laura
Edwards; 4 (right), 25, 45, 48 © Will Heap;
5 (left), 31, 51, 52 © Tara Fisher; 5 (middle
and right), 6–7, 13, 56, 85 © Con Poulos;
10–11, 21, 36–37, 60, 64–65, 81 © Clare
Winfield; 14, 17, 72, 76, 86 © Peter Cassidy;
18, 26, 82, 90 © Gus Filgate; 39, 63 © Dan
Jones; 42, 70 © Georgia Glynn-Smith;
46 © Steve Lee; 59, 75, 89 © Tori Hancock;
69 © Martin Poole; 78 © Eva Kolenko.

Cover photographs: top row, left to right
© Will Heap; Laura Edwards; Will Heap;
Tori Hancock; second row, left to right
© Tara Fisher; Georgia Glynn-Smith;
Tori Hancock; Con Poulos.

Project Editor: Claire Rogers
Designer: Helen Bratby
Illustrator: Jenni Desmond
Production: Nic Jones and Gemma John

A Cataloguing in Publication record
for this title is available from the British
Library.

Colour reproduction by ALTA London
Printed and bound in China by C&C Offset
Printing Co., Ltd.

* Note: all eggs are free-range

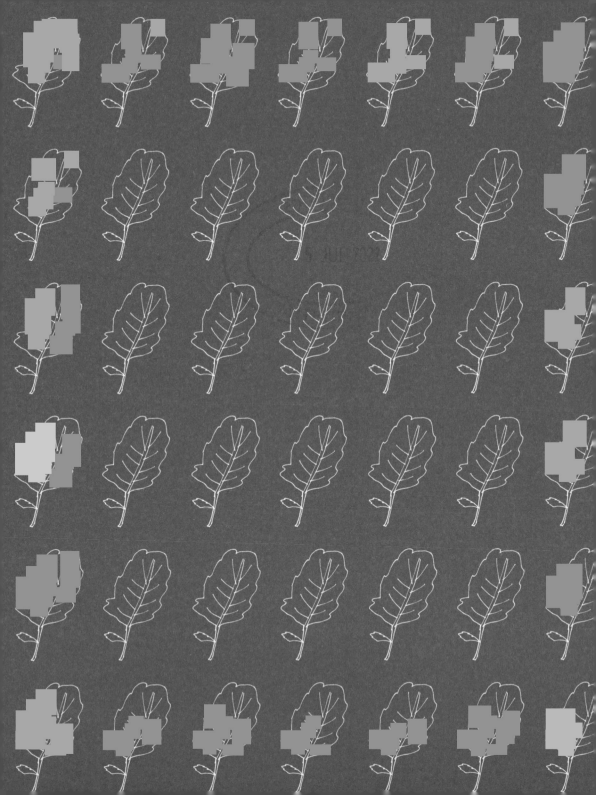